PRESIDENTS IN A TIME OF CHANGE

A SOURCEBOOK ON THE U.S. PRESIDENCY

PRESIDENTS
IN A TIME OF
CHANGE

A SOURCEBOOK ON THE U.S. PRESIDENCY

Edited by Carter Smith

AMERICAN ALBUMS FROM THE COLLECTIONS OF
THE LIBRARY OF CONGRESS

THE MILLBROOK PRESS, *Brookfield, Connecticut*

Cover: President Bill Clinton's inaugural address. Color photograph, January 20, 1993.

Title Page: The Capitol on inauguration day, 1993. Color photograph.

Contents Page: Campaign button for Jimmy Carter, 1976.

Back Cover: Campaign button for Dwight D. Eisenhower, 1956.

3 9082 05690367 0

Library of Congress Cataloging-in-Publication Data

Presidents in a time of change : a sourcebook on the U.S. presidency / edited by Carter Smith.
    p. cm. — (American albums from the collections of the Library of Congress)
    Includes bibliographical references and index.
    Summary: Uses a variety of contemporary materials to describe and illustrate the political and personal lives of the United States presidents from Harry Truman to Bill Clinton.
    ISBN 1-56294-362-6 (lib. bdg.)
    1. Presidents—United States—History—20th century—Juvenile literature. 2. Presidents—United States—History—20th century—Sources—Juvenile literature. 3. United States—Politics and government—1945–1989—Juvenile literature. 4. United States—Politics and government—1945–1989—Sources—Juvenile literature. 5. United States—Politics and government—1989–1993—Juvenile literature. 6. United States—Politics and government—1989–1993—Sources—Juvenile literature. [1. Presidents—Sources. 2. United States—Politics and government—1945–1989—Sources. 3. United States—Politics and government—1989–1993—Sources.] I. Smith, C. Carter. II. Series.
E176.1.P923 1993
973.92'092'2—dc20
[B]
        93-15092
        CIP
        AC

Created in association with Media Projects Incorporated

C. Carter Smith, *Executive Editor*
Lelia Wardwell, *Managing Editor*
Lisa Mirabile, *Principal Writer*
Elizabeth Prince, *Manuscript Editor*
Lydia Link, *Designer*
Athena Angelos, *Picture Researcher*
Shelley Latham, *Researcher*

The consultation of Bernard F. Reilly, Jr., Head Curator of the Prints and Photographs Division of the Library of Congress, is gratefully acknowledged. In addition, the assistance of the research staff at the Truman, Eisenhower, JFK, LBJ, Ford, and Reagan presidential libraries is greatly appreciated.

Manufactured in the United States of America.

10 9 8 7 6 5 4 3 2 1

Contents

Harry S. Truman sits in the Oval Office behind the desk formerly occcupied by Woodrow Wilson. Upon becoming president, Truman requested Woodrow Wilson's desk to replace Roosevelt's. Truman regarded Wilson as the greatest Democratic statesman of the twentieth century.

Introduction

PRESIDENTS IN A TIME OF CHANGE is one of the volumes in a series published by The Millbrook Press titled AMERICAN ALBUMS FROM THE COLLECTIONS OF THE LIBRARY OF CONGRESS and one of six books in the series subtitled SOURCEBOOKS ON THE U.S. PRESIDENCY. This series chronicles the American presidency from George Washington through Bill Clinton.

The works reproduced in this volume reflect the extraordinary wealth of presidential documents held by the Library of Congress. Works from the Library of Congress are supplemented here by others drawn from several presidential libraries, from the White House, and from the Architect of the Capitol.

Presidential libraries exist for every former chief executive since Herbert Hoover. Established by the presidents themselves, their families, or associates, these libraries are administered by the National Archives and Records Administration. They are important centers for the study of the careers and administrations of former chief executives. Many of the libraries, like the LBJ Presidential Library at the University of Texas at Austin, have expanded missions, focusing on large political issues or on the broader sphere of national or world affairs during the president's era. The Library of Congress serves as the *de facto* presidential library for all the presidents before Calvin Coolidge.

Included in presidential library collections are many kinds of pictorial documents, including political cartoons, portraits, family pictures, and photographs of official events, as well as more conventional records such as books and manuscripts. Most of the documents that appear here are photographs, some of them in fact photographs taken of television screens. These images reflect the major role that photojournalism and television have played in shaping public perceptions of American presidents and presidential candidates. During presidential campaigns, the media have become a major preoccupation of those running for office, and the ability to use these powerful forces a highly developed science. Once in the White House, moreover, presidents are now more familiar to American citizens than ever before. No presidential public appearance goes unrecorded by the ever-present camera.

The works reproduced here represent only a small fraction of the thousands of portraits, political cartoons, and other pictorial works that make up the rich record of the American presidency preserved in the Library of Congress and by the presidential libraries in their role as caretakers of the nation's heritage.

BERNARD F. REILLY, JR.

The physical boundaries of the United States (the orange areas on this map) have not changed since 1959, the year Alaska and Hawaii gained statehood. America's role in the world, however, has undergone great changes since the end of World War II. The nation's presidents have become increasingly important in shaping this role through their foreign policy decisions.

In the postwar era, nations clashed not so much over territories or natural wealth as over disagreements in government systems. Starting with the Truman Doctrine of 1947, the U.S. committed itself to supporting any nation struggling against communism. Eisenhower further emphasized America's responsibility as a leader in the new international order, warning against a "fortress America" policy of isolation.

The Cold War introduced new problems when it came in close to America's shores. Two emergency situations developed in Cuba shortly after Kennedy took office: first the Bay of Pigs Invasion and then the Cuban Missile Crisis, which brought the U.S. and the U.S.S.R. to the brink of nuclear war.

The fight against communism close to home continued into the 1980s during Reagan's presidency, first with the invasion of the island of Grenada and then with U.S. government support of anticommunist groups in Central America. When communism collapsed in the late 1980s, America's role as world leader changed yet again. Today, the nations of the world are seeing the need to form a global consensus. Now that the old rivalries have been dissolved the U.S. and other nations can turn their attention to such international concerns as overpopulation and the earth's environment.

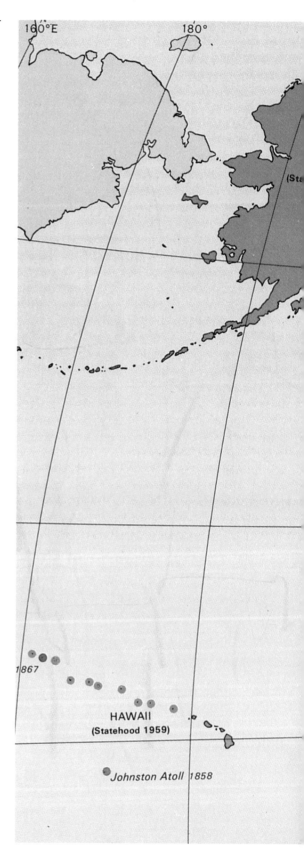

160°E   180°

(St

1867

HAWAII
(Statehood 1959)

Johnston Atoll 1858

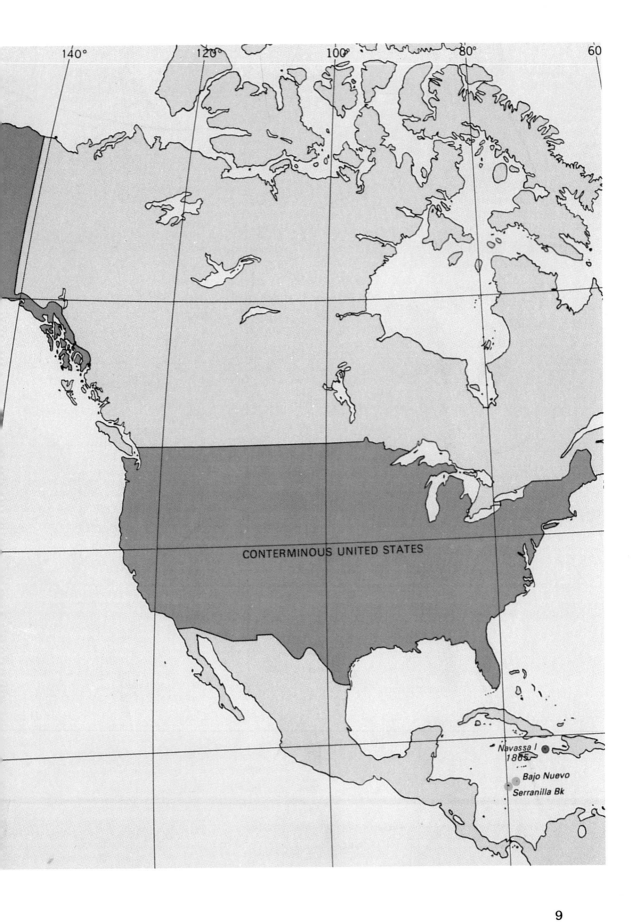

CONTERMINOUS UNITED STATES

Navassa I
1805

Bajo Nuevo

Serranilla Bk

9

THE PRESIDENCY

1945 President Franklin D. Roosevelt dies of a cerebral hemorrhage. Vice President Harry S. Truman becomes the thirty-third president of the United States.

August 6 At the command of President Truman, the first atomic bomb is dropped on Hiroshima, Japan; three days later, a second atomic bomb is dropped on Nagasaki.

August 14 Japan announces unconditional surrender on V-J Day, ending the Second World War.

1947 In a speech to Congress, President Truman spells out the Truman Doctrine. This policy commits the United States to assisting any nation struggling against communism.
• President Truman signs the National Security Act uniting the armed forces under the command of the secretary of defense and creating the National Security Council and the Central Intelligence Agency.
• Congress passes the Presidential Succession Act. The law extends the line of presidential succession to the Speaker of the House of Representatives and the President of the Senate pro tempore, in that order, in the event that both the president and vice president die or are unable to fulfill their duties.

1948 Protesting Truman's support for increased civil rights for African Americans, some Southern Democrats split from the party to form the States Rights Democrats, or "Dixiecrat" party.
• Truman is elected to a second term as president in a surprise victory over Republican Thomas E. Dewey.

THE SCENE AT HOME AND ABROAD

1945 Fifty nations draft and sign the charter of the United Nations at the San Francisco Conference.

1946 Former British prime minister Winston Churchill makes a speech warning of Soviet expansion and coining the phrase, the "Iron Curtain." His speech marks the start of the Cold War between the West and the communist bloc.

• Designed by scientists J. Presper Eckert, Jr., and John Mauchly, the world's first fully electronic digital computer, ENIAC, goes into service.

1947 In a speech at Harvard University, Secretary of State George C. Marshall outlines the European Recovery Program—also known as the Marshall Plan—to help Europe recover from World War II.
• Jackie Robinson joins the Brooklyn Dodgers baseball club. He is the first African-American ballplayer to be accepted into the major leagues.

1948 The United States helps airlift foods and supplies to West Berlin, which has been blockaded by the Soviets in an attempt to force the Western powers to surrender control of the area.

The Berlin Airlift

1949 Truman proposes his Fair Deal program to Congress. The program includes domestic legislation for urban renewal, improved civil rights laws, and the expansion of social security.

1950 President Truman is the target of an assassination attempt by Puerto Rican nationalists. The president is unhurt but a Secret Service agent is killed.

Harry S. Truman

1951 The Twenty-second Amendment to the Constitution is adopted. The amendment sets a two-term limit on the presidency.

1952 World War II hero Dwight D. Eisenhower defeats Democrat Adlai E. Stevenson in the presidential election. Eisenhower is the first Republican president in twenty-four years.
• Fulfilling a campaign promise, President-elect Eisenhower travels to Korea for a three-day tour of

the war zone. Eisenhower's visit is not made public until after his return to the United States.

1956 President Eisenhower signs the Interstate Highway Act for the building of a 42,000-mile highway system across the nation.
• Eisenhower is reelected president of the United States after defeating Democrat candidate Adlai E. Stevenson.

1949 Eleven nations sign the North Atlantic Treaty in Washington, D.C., creating NATO. The treaty states that an armed attack against one or more of the organization members shall be considered an attack against them all.

1950 Senator Joseph A. McCarthy's claim to have the names of 205 known communists in the State Department sets off a nationwide campaign against communists that would last four years.
• The Korean War begins in June when communist North Korea launches a surprise attack on South Korea.
• Ralph J. Bunche, an African American, wins the Nobel Peace Prize for his role in negotiating a peace settlement between the newly-established nation of Israel and its hostile Arab neighbors.
• The census shows that the population

has reached 150 million; 64 percent live in urban areas.

1951 Julius and Ethel Rosenberg are convicted of spying for the Soviet Union. Their execution in 1953 provokes worldwide protest.

1953 The Korean War ends when the two sides sign an armistice agreeing to keep Korea divided.

1954 Physician Jonas Salk develops the injectable

vaccine for polio.
• The U.S. explodes the first hydrogen bomb.

1955 Martin Luther King, Jr., leads an African-American boycott of segregated city buses in Montgomery, Alabama.

1956 Singer Elvis Presley shocks and thrills a record television audience of 54 million people when he performs his hit single "Hound Dog" on Ed Sullivan's show "Talk of the Town."

A TIMELINE OF MAJOR EVENTS

1957–1967

THE PRESIDENCY

1957 President Eisenhower sends federal troops to Central High School in Little Rock, Arkansas, to enforce school desegregation following the Supreme Court's decision in *Brown* v. *The Board of Education of Topeka* in 1954.

1960 Presidential debates are broadcast on television for the first time. Democrat John F. Kennedy wins 49.7 percent of the popular vote to Republican Richard M. Nixon's 49.5 percent.

1961 About 1,500 Cuban exiles trained by the CIA and backed by President Kennedy land at the Bay of Pigs, in Cuba, where they make an unsuccessful attempt to overthrow Premier Fidel Castro.
• President Kennedy establishes the Peace Corps. The organization provides trained volunteers and technical assistance to underdeveloped countries.

1962 When U.S. planes discover Soviet nuclear missile bases in Cuba, President Kennedy demands their removal and announces a blockade on ships going to Cuba. The crisis ends when Soviet premier Nikita Khrushchev agrees to disband the bases.

John F. Kennedy with military advisors

1963 President Kennedy is assassinated by Lee Harvey Oswald in Dallas, Texas, on November 22.

THE SCENE AT HOME AND ABROAD

1958 Regular commercial jet flights begin in the U.S.; Pan-American World Airways begins trans-Atlantic jet service. For the first time, airlines carry more passengers across the Atlantic than ships do.

1959 Alaska and Hawaii are admitted as the forty-ninth and fiftieth states, respectively.

1960 African Americans stage "sit-ins" in the South to force desegregation of lunch counters and other public places.
• According to the U.S. census, the population is nearing 180 million.

1961 The East German government, with the support of the Soviets, seals West Berlin from East Berlin and East Germany. In the following weeks, the "Berlin Wall" is constructed.

• Alan Shepard, Jr., blasts into space aboard a Mercury rocket, becoming the first American astronaut in space.

1962 Andy Warhol leads the pop art movement with his paintings "*Green Coca Cola*" and "*Marilyn Monroe.*"
• Telstar, the first commercial communications satellite, is launched into orbit.
• Rachel Carson's book *Silent Spring*, which describes the damage done to plants, animals, and humans by artifical pesticides, helps launch a growing movement to protect and preserve the earth's environment.

1963 Race riots break out in Harlem, New York City, beginning a five-year period of rioting in urban areas nationwide.
• Representatives of the United States, the Soviet Union, and Great Britain sign a limited nuclear test ban treaty. The docu-

Oswald himself is murdered two days later. Vice President Lyndon B. Johnson becomes the nation's thirty-sixth president.

1964 President Johnson signs the Civil Rights Act of 1964 outlawing discrimination in employment and in public places.
• The Warren Commission, organized to investigate President Kennedy's assassination, issues a report stating that Oswald acted alone

in murdering the president.
• In response to an attack by North Vietnamese vessels on U.S. warships, the Senate passes the Gulf of Tonkin Resolution. The resolution gives the president almost unlimited authority to commit U.S. military forces to South Vietnam in its war against communist North Vietnam.
• Johnson is re-elected president, winning 61 percent of the popular vote to Republican

nominee Barry M. Goldwater's 39 percent.

1965 President Johnson orders the first regular U.S. ground troops to Vietnam.
• Congress passes President Johnson's Voting Rights Act outlawing poll taxes, literacy tests, and other commonly used methods of preventing blacks from voting.

1966 Medicare, a major part of President John-

son's domestic program to establish a "Great Society," begins health insurance coverage for senior citizens.

1967 President Johnson nominates Thurgood Marshall to the Supreme Court. Marshall, famous for his civil rights victories as a lawyer and as U.S. Solicitor General, is the court's first African-American justice.

---

ment bars testing of nuclear devices in the earth's atmosphere, in space, and under water.
• Martin Luther King, Jr., leads a "Freedom March" on Washington, D.C., demanding civil rights for blacks. He delivers his famous "I have a dream . . ." speech to over 200,000 people.

1964 Teamsters president James (Jimmy) Hoffa is convicted of fraud, misuse of union

funds, and jury tampering. He remains president of the Teamsters until 1971, four years after beginning his thirteen-year prison term.
• Civil rights leader

Martin Luther King, Jr., receives the Nobel Peace Prize.

1965 Thirty-five people are killed in race riots in Watts, Los Angeles.

1966 A power struggle in communist China brings the start of the Cultural Revolution. Communist Party chairman Mao Tse-tung directs a purge of bourgeois bureaucrats and communist leaders with Western, capitalistic tendencies.

1967 Race riots claim twenty-six lives in Newark, N.J., and thirty-eight in Detroit.

Martin Luther King, Jr., speaking about civil rights

THE PRESIDENCY

1968 Democratic presidential candidate Robert F. Kennedy is shot and fatally wounded in Los Angeles by Sirhan Bishara Sirhan.

• In a nationally televised speech, President Johnson announces a partial halt to the U.S. bombing of North Vietnam and calls for an end to the increasingly unpopular war. The president stuns the nation by announcing he will not run for another term.

• Richard M. Nixon narrowly defeats Democrat Hubert Humphrey to become the nation's thirty-seventh president. Independent candidate George Wallace wins 14 percent of the popular vote.

1969 President Nixon begins to withdraw troops from Vietnam in a slow process that continues until the U.S. and South Vietnam sign a cease-fire (the Paris Accords) with North Vietnam in 1973.

1972 In a dramatic gesture of good will, President Nixon becomes the first U.S. president to visit communist China.

• President Nixon travels to Moscow to sign the first Strategic Arms Limitation Treaty (SALT). This treaty opens a period of decreased tension (known as détente) between the United States and the Soviet Union.

• Nixon is reelected president of the U.S. by a great majority. Democrat George McGovern wins only one state, Massachusetts, in the electoral college.

1973 Vice President Spiro Agnew resigns, pleading no contest to a charge of tax evasion. Republican congressman Gerald R. Ford is sworn in as his successor.

THE SCENE AT HOME AND ABROAD

1968 North Vietnam launches a major campaign—known as the Tet Offensive—on more than 100 cities, towns, and military bases in South Vietnam.

April 5 Escaped convict James Earl Ray assassinates Martin Luther King, Jr., at Memphis, Tennessee. King's death sparks rioting in nearly 125 cities.

1969 Astronaut Neil Armstrong is the first man to walk on the moon.

• The Woodstock Music and Art Fair takes place near Bethel, N.Y. The festival draws as many as 400,000 people in a celebration that comes to symbolize the youth culture of the 1960s.

1970 Congress establishes the Environmental Protection Agency.

• Four students are killed and nine injured when National Guardsmen open fire on 1,000 antiwar demonstrators at Kent State University in Ohio.

• According to the U.S. census, the population has passed 203 million.

1973 The Arab nations of the Organization of Petroleum Exporting Countries (OPEC) stop selling oil to countries supporting Israel in its war against Egypt and Syria, leading to an energy crisis in the United States.

• In the case of *Roe v. Wade*, the Supreme Court rules that states do not have the right to restrict abortions in most instances. The controversial decision touches off a long-running and emotional national debate about the abortion issue.

1975 The South Vietnamese capital, Saigon, falls to North Vietnamese forces, ending the long Vietnam War. North and South

Impeachment demonstrations

1974 Congress holds televised impeachment hearings against President Nixon after he is charged with conspiring to obstruct justice in the investigation of the Watergate break-in scandal.
• On the verge of impeachment, Nixon becomes the first president in U.S. history to resign. Gerald R. Ford succeeds Nixon and becomes the first American president not elected by the people.
• President Ford grants ex-president Nixon a "full, free and absolute pardon" for crimes he "committed or may have committed" during his presidency.

1975 President Ford survives two assassination attempts in the same month; the president is unhurt in both incidents.

1976 James E. (Jimmy) Carter narrowly defeats Republican Gerald Ford to become the nation's thirty-ninth president.

1978 President Carter launches a campaign for conserving energy.
• With the help of President Carter, Egyptian president Anwar Sadat and Israeli prime minister Menachem Begin negotiate the Camp David Accords, leading to peace after thirty-one years of war.

Vietnam are united under communist rule.

1976 The United States vetoes Vietnam's admission to the U.N. on the grounds that the Hanoi government has not accounted for 800 U.S. servicemen still listed as missing in action.
• The United States celebrates the Bicentennial—the 200th anniversary of the nation's Declaration of Independence from Britain.

1978 A severe financial crisis brings New York, the nation's largest city, to the edge of bankruptcy.

1979 Spurred on by a second oil embargo by OPEC, inflation reaches double digits for the first time in American history.
• Days after the Shah of Iran arrives in New York for medical treatment, an Iranian mob seizes the U.S. Embassy in Teheran, demanding the return of their hated former leader. Fifty-two Americans remain hostage for more than a year.
• An accident at the Three Mile Island nuclear power plant near Harrisburg, Pennsylvania, causes radiation to be released into the atmosphere. It is the worst nuclear accident in American history.

Hostages in Iran

THE PRESIDENCY

1980 Republican Ronald W. Reagan defeats Carter to become the nation's fortieth president. Independent candidate John Anderson wins 7 percent of the popular vote.

Sandra Day O'Connor

1981 On the day of President Reagan's inauguration, the Iranian hostages are freed after 444 days of captivity.
• President Reagan is shot by John W. Hinckley, Jr., while leaving a Washington hotel. Although seriously wounded, Reagan quickly recovers and returns to the White House.
• Sandra Day O'Connor is appointed to the Supreme Court by President Reagan, becoming the first woman to serve on the nation's highest court.

1983 President Reagan authorizes the invasion of the Caribbean island nation of Grenada by U.S. forces to protect American students there after its government is overthrown.

1984 The Reagan administration mines Nicaragua's harbors in its effort to topple that country's procommunist Sandinista government.
• Congress rejects Reagan's request for sending U.S. funds to the Nicaraguan anticommunist "contras."
• Ronald Reagan is reelected president, defeating Democratic candidate Walter F. Mondale by a landslide. Mondale's running mate, Representative Geraldine Ferraro, is the first woman to run for vice president.

THE SCENE AT HOME AND ABROAD

1980 Following the acquittal of four Miami police officers charged with beating to death a black insurance executive, race riots in Miami leave eighteen people dead and property damage of $100 million.
• The census places the population at 226 million. The number of illegal aliens living in America is estimated at 3.5 million.
• An attempt to rescue the Iranian hostages ends in disaster when a helicopter and a transport plane collide in the Iranian desert, killing eight Americans.

1981 The U.S. Center for Disease Control notes what will later be identified as the first cases of Acquired Immune Deficiency Syndrome (AIDS), a deadly (and so far incurable) new disease.
• The national debt passes one trillion dollars.

1983 The U.S. Marine Headquarters in Beirut, Lebanon, is bombed, killing 241 Americans stationed there.
• Soviet forces shoot down a Korean passenger airliner after it strays over Soviet airspace. All 269 passengers are killed.

1984 Researchers discover the virus that causes AIDS.

U.S. marines stationed in Lebanon

1985 President Reagan undergoes surgery to remove a cancerous growth. In a rare case of the transfer of presidential power, Vice President George Bush is briefly acting president.

1986 The Iran-contra scandal breaks out. Members of the Reagan administration are charged with selling arms to Iran in exchange for American hostages held in Lebanon and diverting the funds to support the Nicaraguan contras—a practice that is in direct violation of the Constitution.

1987 Soviet premier Mikhail Gorbachev and President Reagan sign the Intermediate-Range Nuclear Forces (INF) treaty.

1988 Vice President George H. W. Bush defeats Democrat Michael S. Dukakis to become the nation's forty-first president.

1989 President Bush sends U.S. forces into Panama to oust Panamanian president Manuel Noriega and bring him to the U.S. to stand trial for drug trafficking.

1990 Iraqi president Saddam Hussein invades Kuwait, jeopardizing world oil interests. With the help of the United Nations, President Bush organizes an international coalition against Iraq.

1992 President Bush sends U.S. troops to drought- and war-ravaged Somalia to protect relief food deliveries from looters.
• Democrat William (Bill) Clinton defeats George Bush to become the forty-second president. A third candidate, billionaire H. Ross Perot, wins 19 percent of the popular vote in his call for major economic and political reforms.

1985 Mikhail Gorbachev, the new general secretary of the Soviet Union, calls for far-reaching change in his country.

1986 The space shuttle *Challenger* explodes on take-off, killing all seven people aboard, including the first non-astronaut to fly into space, teacher Christa McAuliffe.
• U.S. warplanes attack Libya, hoping to disrupt its terrorist activities.

1987 The New York stock market suffers the worst one-day decline since the stock market crash of 1929. The crash sets off a nationwide economic recession.

1989 A series of mostly peaceful revolutions free the Soviet-bloc nations of Eastern Europe from communist control; the Berlin Wall, separating East and West Berlin, is torn down.
• In a massive environmental disaster, the tanker *Exxon Valdez* goes aground on the Alaskan coast, spilling more than 1 million gallons of oil into Prince William Sound.

1990 Military hard-liners attempt to overthrow Soviet president Mikhail Gorbachev. Although the coup fails, it leads to the end of the Soviet Union.

1992 The worst race riots in U.S. history break out in Los Angeles after four white police officers are acquitted in the brutal beating of Rodney King, a black man. The riots result in fifty-two deaths and over $1 billion in property damage.

1993 The World Trade Center in New York City is bombed in a terrorist attack leaving 5 dead and hundreds injured. Islamic militants are believed to be responsible.

Part I
The Cold War Years

As the nation grew larger and more complex after World War II, the power of the executive branch grew with it. The president's role, as defined by the Constitution, had not changed since that document was ratified in 1788. But under Franklin D. Roosevelt, whose New Deal enlarged the government's role in people's daily lives, the Constitution was interpreted to give broader powers to the executive branch. In particular, the president was given power to set up the new agencies and regulations that were required by a larger government.

In addition, the president's role as the chief architect of the nation's foreign policy became more prominent during the ensuing period of the Cold War. The Cold War was caused by dueling political systems—communism and democracy—and on the military might of the world's two "superpowers," the Soviet Union and the United States. The Soviet Union waged an international campaign to convert other countries to communism and Soviet rule, often by force. The United States became concerned that a Soviet empire, backed by massive nuclear arsenals, would destroy democracy throughout the world. It fell to the president to negotiate with Soviet leadership to ease these tensions and forge a more peaceable path.

The outcome of the growth of executive power was, in some ways, predictable. The executive branch overstepped its bounds, upsetting the delicate balance of powers established by the Constitution. The Watergate scandal, although caused by the misdeeds of the Nixon administration, stemmed in part from a growing presidential belief that the president ruled the nation on his own.

Preparing to leave the White House after being forced to resign from office, Richard Nixon (left) signals the White House staff with his signature "V" for victory sign.

HARRY TRUMAN: EARLY YEARS

Harry S. Truman was born to Martha and John Truman on May 8, 1884, in Lamar, Missouri. "S" was his full middle name, standing for his two grandfathers, Solomon Young and Shippe Truman. (Truman did not in fact punctuate his middle name.) Growing up in Independence, Missouri, Truman was a quiet boy who liked to read. He also became an accomplished pianist. Truman graduated from high school in 1901 and immediately went to work, since his father had recently gone bankrupt. After a series of odd jobs, he returned in 1906 to run the family farm in Grandview, Missouri. In 1917, as the nation geared up to enter World War I, Truman rejoined the Missouri National Guard (where he had served from 1905–11). After the U.S. entered the war, Truman's unit became part of the army, where he served full-time until May 1919.

After the war, Truman married Elizabeth (Bess) Wallace (1885–1982), his childhood sweetheart, and opened a hat shop in Kansas City. The shop was successful at first but went bankrupt in 1922. It took Truman twelve years to pay off all his debts.

Later in 1922, Truman was elected judge of the Eastern District of Jackson County, an administrative post, and the following year he began law school. In 1926 he was elected presiding judge of the county. He remained in that office until 1934, when he won a seat in the U.S. Senate.

Harry Truman (above) wore eyeglasses from an early age. Since glasses were very expensive when he was a child, he was not allowed to play many sports. Bad vision later prevented Truman from being admitted to West Point.

Truman, as a young man, stands with his mother and grandmother at the family farm in Grandview, Missouri (right). The family moved to the farm in 1906. Harry oversaw it until 1917, when he left to serve in the army during World War I.

Captain Harry Truman (right) poses in his uniform of the 129th Field Artillery. Truman entered the army as a lieutenant. He was promoted to captain soon after his arrival in France, in March of 1918. While in France, Truman commanded the 129th's Battery D, which saw active combat several times before the end of the war.

TRUMAN: SUCCESSION TO THE PRESIDENCY

Truman's successful political career resulted in part from his association with the powerful but corrupt Missouri politician Thomas J. Pendergast, whose son he had known during the war. Unlike "Boss" Pendergast, however, Truman was an honest politician and soon won the respect of his peers in the Senate. A loyal Democrat, he supported the controversial New Deal policies of President Franklin D. Roosevelt (1882–1945) and was reelected to a second Senate term in 1940.

Truman came to national attention during World War II when he chaired a committee that uncovered billions of dollars of waste in the defense budget. In 1944 President Roosevelt, who was running for a record fourth term, asked Truman to be his new running mate. Although the senator was reluctant, he eventually gave in to Roosevelt's pressure. The Roosevelt–Truman ticket won, 53 to 46 percent over Republican nominee Thomas Dewey (1902–71).

On the evening of April 12, 1945, only a little more than two months after taking office, Vice President Truman was called to the White House. There, Mrs. Roosevelt told him the president had died. Within hours, Truman became the thirty-third president of the United States.

Elizabeth Virginia Wallace (above), known as Bess, was born and raised in Independence, Missouri. Truman and Bess met in early childhood, but took their time courting. They only became romantically attached in their late twenties, and married when he was thirty-five and she was thirty-four.

Harry S. Truman and Franklin D. Roosevelt (right) talk campaign strategy for Roosevelt's unprecedented fourth bid for the presidency in 1944. After the meeting, Truman voiced concern about Roosevelt's physical weakness. The president had found it difficult to steady even a small creamer of milk.

Senator Truman (right) poses here in front of the U.S. Capitol. During his ten years as a senator from Missouri, Truman served on the Appropriations Committee and the Interstate Commerce Committee.

THE FIRST COLD WAR PRESIDENT

Germany surrendered less than a month after Truman took office, but the war with Japan raged on. Truman decided to use the new atomic bomb to speed the end of the Pacific war. The bombing of the Japanese cities of Hiroshima and Nagasaki—which killed more than 120,000 civilians and leveled the two cities—was perhaps the most historic—and controversial—presidential decision of the century.

The new president took a tough stand toward the Soviet Union. At the war's end, Soviet leader Joseph Stalin (1879–1953) had acted quickly to impose communist governments in eastern Europe. In a March 1947 speech, Truman promised U.S. support to any nation struggling against communism. Called the Truman Doctrine, this anticommunist pledge would define U.S. foreign policy for decades.

As soon as the war ended, Truman showed himself to be a reformer who intended to build on the New Deal. Although very little of his so-called "Fair Deal" program ever passed Congress, Truman aimed to ensure every citizen a decent place to live, a good education, a job, and health care.

Few people expected Truman to win a second term in 1948. Thomas Dewey, the popular governor of New York, was again the Republican nominee. But Truman waged an energetic campaign, warning that the Republicans wanted to undo Roosevelt's New Deal and blaming a "do nothing" Congress for many of the nation's ills. Against all odds, he won.

President Truman sits between British prime minister Winston Churchill and Soviet premier Joseph Stalin (above) at the Potsdam Conference on August 2, 1945. It was here that Truman first heard of the successful testing of the atomic bomb.

This drawing (right) summarizes Truman's energetic 1948 presidential campaign. Truman traveled 32,000 miles and made hundreds of off-the-cuff, "whistle-stop" speeches in which he attacked the "do-nothing" Republican-led Congress. A cheering public greeted the president in large crowds, calling for Truman to "Give 'em Hell!" in Washington.

TRUMAN: SECOND TERM AND LATER YEARS

In the 1948 election, the Democrats also regained control of both houses of Congress, recovering from a dramatic Republican victory in 1946. Nevertheless, Truman's Fair Deal continued to stall. The president did eventually win a higher minimum wage, an important federal housing act, and a broadened Social Security system. But Congress never passed any of his major reforms, such as national health insurance or a civil rights bill.

The Fair Deal was a victim of the growing Cold War. The fight against communism continued to dominate Truman's administration. In June 1950, communist North Korea invaded pro-Western South Korea. Truman rallied the newly created United Nations to assemble a force—mostly American—to help South Korea drive the communists back. But the war turned into a long and frustrating stalemate.

Despite Truman's upset victory in the 1948 election, his popularity was never high, and it sagged lower as the Korean War dragged on. The president announced that he would not seek a third term. (The Twenty-second Amendment, limiting future presidents to two terms, became law in 1951.) Truman retired to Independence, Missouri, but remained an active member of the Democratic Party well into the 1960s. He died on December 26, 1972.

In the late 1940s, consumers began crying out over soaring inflation. This cartoon (below), published in the New York Mirror *in September 1952, criticizes Truman's Fair Deal program for higher wages and better working conditions. The cartoonist presents the Fair Deal as a movie set propped up only by inflation and war spending, while a crowd of enthusiastic workers gathers to hear more about the program.*

President Truman greets General Douglas MacArthur (above), who headed the U.N. forces assembled to help South Korea. When China entered the war on North Korea's side, MacArthur strongly urged Truman to extend the war to China. Truman choose not to do so. When MacArthur publicly opposed this decision, Truman fired the extremely popular general, stirring tremendous controversy.

These "Red Wing" apples were sent to Wisconsin senator Joseph McCarthy (right; 1908–57) in 1953 by the staff of a Canadian newspaper. The paper's editorial board, disgusted by McCarthy's vicious and unfounded attacks on supposed "communists" in government and private industry, told him, "Here is something for you and your committee to dig your teeth in. The woods are full of them." McCarthy's crusade had a lasting impact on foreign-policy debate during Truman's presidency.

The House Un-American Activities Committee, in session in this photograph (below), unleashed a furor of anticommunist activity. The committee, under Republican control from 1947, sought to discredit Truman's administration by proving that the Democrats were "soft" on communism and had allowed spies to penetrate the government.

Truman was an accomplished pianist; as a teenager, he briefly contemplated a career in music. In a tribute to the former president, comedian Jack Benny taped a special for his television variety show at the Truman Library in Independence, where he accompanied the former president in a duet (right).

Harry and Bess Truman had only one child, a daughter they named Margaret, born in 1924. They pose (below) with Margaret, her husband, Clifton Daniel, Jr., a reporter for The New York Times, and three of their four grandsons—Harrison (in Truman's lap), William (in front of Margaret), and Clifton Truman (far right).

EISENHOWER: EARLY YEARS

The last U.S. president born in the nineteenth century, David Dwight Eisenhower (he later switched his first two names), was born to David and Ida Eisenhower on October 14, 1890, in Denison, Texas. Soon after his birth, the family moved to Abilene, Kansas, where Dwight grew up as a cheerful, athletic boy. An average student, Eisenhower graduated from Abilene High School in 1909 and from West Point in 1915.

As a new lieutenant, Eisenhower was posted at Fort Sam Houston, in Texas. Although he requested overseas duty during World War I, Eisenhower was assigned duties in the U.S. On July 1, 1916, he married Marie "Mamie" Doud, whom he had met at Fort Sam Houston the previous October.

Eisenhower was an able soldier, and his army rank rose steadily. He received several temporary wartime promotions and became a permanent major in 1920. In 1935 he was finally posted overseas, to the Philippines. He served there as an aide to General Douglas MacArthur, whose staff he had joined in 1932. Eisenhower returned to the United States in 1940, and in 1941 he was promoted to full colonel and then to brigadier general as the United States prepared to enter World War II.

Young Eisenhower (above, foreground) enjoys a camping trip with friends in 1907. Eisenhower was an active, athletic boy. He played football and baseball in high school, and continued to play football at West Point. His athletic career ended in his second year there, however, when he injured his knee so badly he could never play football again.

Cadet Dwight David Eisenhower (above)
poses at West Point. Eisenhower chose
West Point in part because his family was
too poor to pay for college. Although he
graduated a lackluster sixty-first out of a
class of 164, in 1926 he placed first in his
class of 275 at the prestigious Command
and General Staff School, a sub-division of
the academy.

This pilot's license (left) was issued to
Eisenhower on November 30, 1939, near
the end of his tour of duty in the Philippines. Eisenhower, the first president to
earn a pilot's license, made his first solo
flight on May 19, 1937.

SUPREME COMMANDER

After America entered World War II in December 1941, Eisenhower was posted to Washington, D.C., as an assistant chief of staff. He was promoted to major general only months later. In June, Eisenhower was named commander of U.S. forces in Europe, and shortly afterward became the commander in chief of the Allied forces in North Africa. In this position, he orchestrated the invasions of North Africa, Sicily, and mainland Italy.

At the end of 1943, Eisenhower, now a full general, became the supreme commander of the Allied Expeditionary Force. He was in charge of organizing the final invasion of Europe, which led to the conquest of Germany in May 1945.

After the war, Eisenhower returned to Washington as the army's chief of staff. In 1948, after more than thirty years in the army, he resigned to become president of Columbia University. But Eisenhower did not find academic life particularly fulfilling, and after two years at Columbia (most of which he spent on leave, helping to organize the new Department of Defense), Eisenhower returned to the military as supreme commander of the new North Atlantic Treaty Organization (NATO), an alliance of nations formed in the aftermath of World War II. The alliance included Britain, France, and the United States, among others. NATO allies agreed to view an attack on any member nation as an attack against all, and to act as a united political and military body.

On June 6, 1944, Allied commander in chief Eisenhower rallied paratroopers of the 101st Airborne Division. Eisenhower called for "Full victory—nothing else," as the paratroopers boarded planes for the final invasion of Europe (above).

Eisenhower was a reluctant presidential nominee—so secretive was his political affiliation that for years President Truman had hoped Eisenhower would succeed him as the Democratic nominee. But once Eisenhower declared as a Republican, party leaders (including Massachusetts senator Henry Cabot Lodge, who became Eisenhower's campaign manager) encouraged Eisenhower's shift from military to political life, symbolized by the "civvies" in this cartoon (right).

YOUR NEW CLOTHES, GENERAL!

CIVVIES

LODGE

LUTE PEASE

EISENHOWER: FIRST TERM

In 1952, Eisenhower defeated conservative Ohio senator Robert Taft to win the Republican party's presidential nomination and chose California senator Richard Nixon as his vice-presidential nominee. In the election, Eisenhower beat Democratic nominee Adlai Stevenson by a resounding 55 to 44 percent.

Eisenhower's popularity did not win the Republicans a majority in Congress, however, and the new president neither sought nor achieved major domestic reforms. Instead, he consolidated the powers of the modern presidency and offered the nation a chance to absorb the changes that the New Deal, World War II, and postwar world leadership had brought about. Perhaps his most important achievement was convincing the nation to shoulder its international burden as leader of the free world, rather than trying to create a "fortress America"—one shielded from outside responsibilities—as leading conservatives wished to do.

The Cold War dominated Eisenhower's two terms in office. Eisenhower believed that a strong defense was the best way to avoid war with the Soviet Union and oversaw the buildup of U.S. nuclear weapons. But he had no wish to engage in an arms race, and actually cut the defense budget by $10 billion—a full one fifth.

The famous "I Like Ike" campaign button (above) captured the reason for much of Eisenhower's success as a politician: Americans liked him. He certainly didn't win on the strength of his political involvement; when his name was mentioned as a possible presidential candidate in 1948, it was discovered that he had never voted because he felt soldiers had a duty to remain above politics.

Eisenhower (right), supreme commander of NATO, waves from the plane as he returns from Paris in 1951. One reason Eisenhower decided to run for president in 1952 was in order to maintain the nation's commitment to a new international order—something Robert Taft, his primary challenger for the nomination, vowed to undo.

Marie Geneva Doud (right), known as Mamie, was considered a formidable First Lady among the White House staff. Servants were not allowed to use the family elevator. She even refused to allow a servant to walk through the White House to get from one wing to another—servants had to enter from an outside entrance.

SECOND TERM AND LATER YEARS

Although Eisenhower suffered a heart attack in September 1955, his recovery was good, and he decided to seek a second term in 1956. He won renomination as the Republican candidate easily, and once again faced Adlai Stevenson as the Democratic nominee. This time, he beat Stevenson by an even larger margin. Still, Eisenhower's tremendous popular support did not lead to any radical reforms.

One of the most important domestic actions of Eisenhower's presidency came in the field of civil rights. A historic Supreme Court ruling had ordered public schools to desegregate in 1954, but many school districts in the South resisted. In Little Rock, Arkansas, the resistance turned violent in the fall of 1957. Eisenhower, preferring diplomacy to force, met with Arkansas governor Orval Faubus to ask him to uphold the law. Faubus refused. Nine black students were turned away from the white high school by a violent mob. The next day, Eisenhower sent federal troops to guarantee the students' safety and their right to education in an integrated school. This forceful action established once and for all that the federal government could, and would, enforce Supreme Court rulings on education and civil rights issues.

In 1961, Eisenhower retired to Gettysburg, Pennsylvania, where he and Mamie lived in their first permanent home after twenty-eight moves during his career. He died of heart failure on March 28, 1969.

Eisenhower (above) greets the 1960 Democratic president-elect, John F. Kennedy. Eisenhower, the only Republican president elected between 1931 and 1968, represented the moderate wing of his party. Although he certainly slowed the rapid pace of domestic reform, he was not opposed to change. Many Americans drive daily on one lasting reminder of his presidency: We owe our extensive interstate highway system to a bill he signed in 1956.

Eisenhower poses for a family portrait (right) in Palm Desert, California: (from left) Anne, brother Milton, Mamie, Joe Carlson, Susan, Dwight David Eisenhower, grandson David, son John, Mary, and Barbara Eisenhower.

KENNEDY:
EARLY YEARS

Born on May 29, 1917, to Joseph and Rose Kennedy, John Fitzgerald Kennedy was the second of nine children in a wealthy Irish Catholic family. As a boy and as an adult, he was athletic and competitive. He was also sickly, however. Among other things, he suffered from a bad back throughout his life. Kennedy attended private schools and entered Princeton University in 1935, but withdrew due to illness. He later attended Harvard, where he earned a degree in 1940. During his junior year, he spent time in England with his father, the U.S. ambassador there. His senior thesis about England's decision not to challenge Hitler in Munich in 1939 was published under the title *Why England Slept* (1940).

Kennedy was unable to join the army due to his weak back, but he finally joined the navy in September 1941. With help from his father, Kennedy eventually became commander of PT-109, a torpedo boat. Kennedy earned several medals for his actions when PT-109 was attacked by the Japanese, but the incident injured his back and ended his military career.

After the war, Kennedy entered politics. In 1946, he won election to Congress as a Democratic representative from Massachusetts at the remarkably young age of twenty-nine. In 1956, Kennedy published *Profiles in Courage*, an account of eight U.S. senators. The book was awarded the Pulitzer Prize.

This picture shows a youthful John F. Kennedy (above) on vacation in Germany. Kennedy was born in Brookline, Massachusetts (an affluent suburb of Boston), where he lived until about age nine. Then the family moved to New York. The Kennedy family always remained loyal to Massachusetts, however, and returned every summer to their home in Hyannis Port, on Cape Cod. Kennedy later represented the state of his birth, first in the House of Representatives and later in the Senate.

The Kennedy family sits for a happy family portrait on a summer's day in Hyannis Port (opposite, top). Although wealthy, the family was not entirely blessed: One daughter, Rosemary, was mentally retarded, and three sons and a daughter were killed in their prime. Joe Jr. was killed in action during World War II; Kathleen died in an airplane accident; and Jack and Bobby were both assassinated.

Young Lieutenant Kennedy stands at the helm of PT 109 (right), the navy torpedo boat he commanded in the Pacific during World War II. In August 1943 the boat was rammed by a Japanese ship. Despite a painful back injury, Kennedy swam for four hours—towing an injured crew member—to the safety of an island. He and the remaining crew were rescued a few days later.

KENNEDY AND THE NEW FRONTIER

Kennedy won reelection to the House twice. In 1952, in his first bid for the Senate, he faced the formidable Republican senator Henry Cabot Lodge, but won by a narrow margin of 70,000 votes. That September, Kennedy married Jacqueline Bouvier, whom he had met two years before.

Kennedy was a popular senator. He handily won reelection to his Senate seat in 1958, but soon turned his attention to even higher goals. Two years later, when he was barely forty-three, he won the Democratic nomination for president.

The 1960 presidential campaign, which pitted Kennedy against Vice President Richard Nixon, was notable in several ways. In the first televised debate between presidential candidates, Kennedy's youth and vigor gave him a decisive edge. The TV audience awarded him the first debate, while radio listeners judged Nixon the winner. In addition, Kennedy was a Roman Catholic. Some voters charged that Kennedy's first allegiance would be to Rome, not to the American people. In response, the candidate openly asked, "Would you deny a man the chance to serve his country on the basis of his faith?"

Kennedy promised to "get the country moving again" after the sluggish Eisenhower years. His plan, called the New Frontier, included stronger civil rights laws, medical care for the elderly, and increased aid for education.

John and Jackie Kennedy (above) pose at their wedding on September 12, 1953. Kennedy, long considered one of the capital city's most eligible bachelors, did not marry until he was thirty-six. His new wife was twenty-four.

John Kennedy and his brother Robert (opposite, top), manager of Kennedy's presidential campaign, await news of Kennedy's nomination at the Democratic National Convention in July 1960. Kennedy's main rival for the nomination was Lyndon B. Johnson, a moderate Southerner whom Kennedy chose as his vice-presidential running mate.

Kennedy delivers his landmark inaugural address (right), the most famous of all his speeches. In it, he demanded: "Ask not what your country can do for you; ask what you can do for your country."

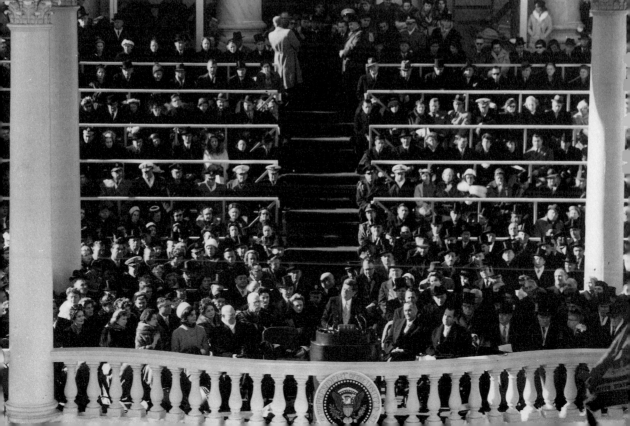

KENNEDY: CRISES

Kennedy seized power energetically. But he faced a foreign-policy disaster only a few months after taking office. On April 17, 1961, a small force of CIA-trained Cuban exiles invaded Cuba, aiming to spark a popular revolution to topple the communist government of Fidel Castro. The scheme, called the Bay of Pigs Invasion, had been planned by the CIA and approved by President Eisenhower. Once in office, Kennedy had given the mission the go-ahead. The popular uprising never came, however, and Kennedy, cutting his losses, refused to send U.S. forces to back up the rebels, who met a humiliating defeat.

That August, the Cold War flared again when East Germany built a wall dividing east Berlin from west Berlin. In October 1962, relations between the United States and the Soviet Union came to a dangerous head: A spy satellite had discovered a Soviet missile base under construction in Cuba. In the defining moment of his presidency, Kennedy demanded that Soviet leader Nikita Khrushchev remove the missiles, and intercepted all ships headed toward Cuba. Khrushchev eventually removed the missiles, but it was the closest the world had ever come to nuclear war.

Meanwhile, in Southeast Asia, communist forces threatened to take control of both Laos and South Vietnam. Kennedy eventually sent thousands of military advisors to South Vietnam, beginning the nation's disastrous commitment to what would become the Vietnam War.

Like her husband, Jacqueline Bouvier Kennedy (above) was raised in a wealthy family. Jackie brought elegance and style to the White House; it was rumored that the French president and World War II hero Charles De Gaulle was in love with her. Her popularity was a political asset for her husband, whose administration was often plagued by international turmoil.

President Kennedy talks with Soviet leader Nikita Khrushchev (opposite, top). The relationship between these two men—leaders of the world's superpowers—was a crucial one, but it got off to a bad start. After the disaster at the Bay of Pigs, Khrushchev decided that Kennedy was indecisive and could be bullied. It was a misunderstanding that almost led to war during the Cuban missile crisis in October 1962.

Despite the very real threat to their homeland, Cuban Americans supported President Kennedy during the Cuban missile crisis, as this photo taped on a Cuban-owned storefront (right) in Miami shows.

THE KENNEDY DYNASTY

John F. Kennedy was the first president to appoint a sibling to a cabinet post when his younger brother, Robert Francis Kennedy (1925–68), was selected as United States attorney general. The appointment was greeted with outrage from much of the public. In editorials, the press charged Kennedy with nepotism, where family members or close friends are favored for important positions. The president, however, was glib and definite in his response, saying, "I see nothing wrong with giving Robert some legal experience before he goes out to practice law." Having successfully managed JFK's campaigns for the Senate and the presidency, Bobby Kennedy quickly became the president's most trusted advisor.

This unique political alliance was cut tragically short on November 22, 1963, the day President Kennedy was assassinated at a parade in Dallas.

A grieving Bobby Kennedy continued in his post as attorney general until 1964, when he returned to politics. Elected senator from New York, Kennedy continued in his brother's footsteps. In 1968, he announced his bid for the presidency.

Bobby Kennedy died from an assassin's bullet, on June 6, 1968. His assassin, Sirhan B. Sirhan, narrowly avoided the death penalty after the Kennedy family pleaded for his life, calling for "an end to the violence."

John and Robert Kennedy (above) were an extraordinary example of cooperation between siblings. The whole Kennedy family was politically exceptional: Three brothers—John, Robert, and Edward (Ted)— were all elected to the Senate, among their other accomplishments.

As chief counsel for the Senate Labor Rackets Committee, Robert Kennedy (right, with brother Jack) oversaw the hearings that led to the racketeering conviction of Dave Beck, president of the Teamsters Union. Afterward, Kennedy swore that he would jump off the Capitol building if he couldn't convict Jimmy Hoffa, who succeeded Beck. Hoffa, however, was ultimately acquitted.

KENNEDY'S
ASSASSINATION

On November 22, 1963, President Kennedy and his wife traveled to Dallas, Texas, in preparation for the upcoming presidential campaign. There, while riding in an open limousine, the president was shot and killed by Lee Harvey Oswald.

A stunned nation grieved deeply for this young president, who had promised to do so much to change the world. The tragedy of his assassination, however, fueled a myth about Kennedy; for a time, he appeared to many to have been an almost perfect president. Recently, historians and scholars have offered a more balanced view of Kennedy. Many of his political ambitions, such as the New Frontier, were accomplished only after his death, when Kennedy's successor, Lyndon Johnson, was able to mobilize a grieving nation. In addition, disclosures about Kennedy's personal life, particularly his relationships with several women, have tarnished his reputation as a perfect president.

Before Oswald could be tried and his motives uncovered, Oswald himself was killed by Jack Ruby, a Dallas nightclub owner. To this day, many people believe that President Kennedy was the victim of a massive conspiracy, although the Warren Commission, appointed by President Johnson to investigate the murder, found that Oswald had acted alone.

The image of the flag-draped coffin (right) of the slain president is a memory printed indelibly in the minds of many Americans. Kennedy's funeral was modeled after President Abraham Lincoln's: Mrs. Kennedy researched all the details and repeated many of the arrangements exactly.

Lee Harvey Oswald (below), the alleged assassin of President Kennedy, is taken into custody by federal authorities in Dallas. Less than forty-eight hours after the president's assassination, Oswald was gunned down by Jack Ruby, a Dallas nightclub owner, during a routine escort through a narrow jail corridor. His murder was broadcast live on televisions throughout the nation.

Jackie and brother-in-law Robert (right) watch as Kennedy's coffin passes. Mrs. Kennedy appeared on television shortly after the funeral to thank all those who had sent their condolences. She was praised throughout the world for her extreme poise and quiet grace.

JOHNSON: EARLY YEARS

Lyndon Baines Johnson was born to Samuel and Rebekah Johnson on August 27, 1908, near Johnson City, Texas. After graduating from high school in 1924, Johnson spent three years traveling before he attended Southwest Texas State Teachers College, where he earned a degree in 1930.

Johnson spent a year teaching before he entered politics as secretary to Congressman Richard Kleberg, a Texas Democrat. He was appointed by President Roosevelt to direct the National Youth Administration in Texas, where he helped young people find jobs during the Depression. In 1934, Johnson met and married Claudia "Lady Bird" Taylor (1912–).

In 1937, Johnson won a seat in Congress, representing the tenth district of Texas for the next twelve years. During his tenure, Johnson served in the U.S. Navy from December 1941 to July 1942, and earned a Silver Star. He resigned when President Roosevelt requested that congressmen return to their duties in Washington.

Johnson was an enthusiastic supporter of Roosevelt and the New Deal, and in 1948 he narrowly won a seat in the Senate. Johnson rose quickly to power, becoming the Democratic whip. (A whip is the Democrat or Republican responsible for insuring discipline and attendance within party ranks.) Johnson later became Senate minority leader, and then majority leader (the youngest in history, at forty-six) when the Democrats regained control of Congress in 1955.

*Johnson poses with students at the Wel-
hausen School in Cotulla, Texas in this photograph (above). Johnson taught at this predomi-
nately Mexican-American school in 1928–29
while earning his teaching degree.*

*Unlike John F. Kennedy, Lyndon Johnson
came from a modest rural background. As
a boy growing up in Texas, Johnson (left)
worked at many different jobs to earn extra
money. He worked his way through college as,
among other things, a garbage collector.*

*Lyndon Johnson practiced his profession only
briefly—he spent one year as a teacher before
entering politics. In fact, while in college
Johnson not only participated in campus politics but also ran the campaign of a state senator and attended the 1928 Democratic
National Convention. Shown here is Johnson's
state teaching certificate (right).*

Teachers Permanent Certificate
The Department of Education
State of Texas

Mr. *Lyndon Baines Johnson*

having presented satisfactory evidence of good moral character, and
having fulfilled the requirements prescribed by law, is now granted
this *Permanent High School* state certificate,
which entitles him to teach in *all grades*
of the public schools of Texas.   This certificate is valid during the
life of the holder, unless revoked by lawful authority.

Date of issue *August 21,* 19 *30*

State Superintendent of Public Instruction.

SEAL

REQUIREMENTS

____approved college degree with teaching
experience and professional courses.

6 years approved teachers college training.

JOHNSON: SUCCESSION TO THE PRESIDENCY

Although Johnson consistently voted against the expansion of civil rights in his early political career, his support as Senate leader was crucial to the passage of the civil rights acts of 1957 and 1960. In 1960, Johnson ran for the Democratic presidential nomination against John F. Kennedy. He lost, but, in a move that surprised many, Kennedy asked Johnson to be his vice-presidential running mate. Although liberals were dismayed by Kennedy's choice of a moderate Southern Democrat, Johnson probably gave Kennedy the winning margin in several key Southern states.

As vice president, Johnson served as chairman of the Committee on Equal Employment Opportunity and the National Aeronautics and Space Administration (NASA). NASA was charged with filling President Kennedy's promise to put a man on the moon by the end of the decade. Johnson was active in representing the United States abroad, and gained popularity for an effective visit to West Berlin in 1961, just after the Berlin Wall was built.

Johnson was riding two cars behind Kennedy when the president was assassinated on November 22, 1963; he was sworn in as the thirty-sixth president less than two hours after Kennedy's death.

Claudia Alta Taylor (above), known as Lady Bird since childhood, met Lyndon Johnson in 1934, at the age of twenty-one. She evidently swept Johnson completely off his feet, for he proposed the day after they met. Lady Bird is best remembered for her efforts to clean up America: The 1965 Highway Beautification Act she supported limited the number of billboards along highways.

Aboard Air Force One, federal judge Sarah Hughes administers the oath of office to a somber Lyndon Johnson (opposite, top) as Mrs. Kennedy looks on.

President Johnson looks skeptical in this photograph (right) of a meeting with Martin Luther King, Jr. In fact, Johnson did more to aid the civil rights effort than any president in history. He was especially proud of the Voting Rights Act of 1965, which outlawed literacy tests and other means of preventing blacks from voting.

THE VIETNAM WAR

Working quickly to heal the nation's grief and anger, Johnson declared a war on poverty in his 1964 State of the Union address. The best known successes of Johnson's "Great Society" include the establishment of Medicare and Medicaid; the Civil Rights Act of 1964, which outlawed racial discrimination in employment and segregation in hotels and restaurants; and the Head Start program, which provided early educational assistance to children of poor families. In the 1964 election, Johnson won easily over the strongly conservative Republican candidate, Barry M. Goldwater.

In August 1964, the Vietnamese allegedly fired on two U.S. ships in the Gulf of Tonkin. In response, Congress granted Johnson broad power to "prevent further aggression." Despite his campaign stance as the candidate for peace, Johnson began air raids over North Vietnam in February 1965.

On January 31, 1968, the North Vietnamese launched the Tet Offensive (named for the Vietnamese New Year holiday). The North Vietnamese sent troops into, among other places, Saigon, where their mission was to destroy the new American embassy building. American and South Vietnamese troops were caught completely by surprise. Although the communists were defeated militarily and the embassy was saved, the Viet Cong won a more important victory. The Tet Offensive proved that, despite government promises, the war's end was not just around the corner.

U.S. helicopters from the 1st Cavalry land in a Vietnamese rice paddy on a search-and-destroy mission in this photograph (right). Vietnam was the first televised war, and scenes like this would become all too familiar to American families watching the war from home. Many military leaders felt that the press coverage severely undermined the war effort.

This heated confrontation between anti-war protesters and police (below) was a familiar sight in the late 1960s. The anti-war movement received so much media attention that when American troops were finally withdrawn from Vietnam, some military officials blamed the press for "losing the war."

JOHNSON: END OF PRESIDENCY AND LAST YEARS

As U.S. involvement in Vietnam grew, so did popular resistance. Johnson's popularity plummeted in the face of growing protests against the Vietnam War. During the New Hampshire primary for the 1968 Democratic presidential nomination, Johnson was almost defeated by Minnesota senator Eugene McCarthy, who was strongly pro-peace. In a surprise announcement in March, Johnson declared that he would not run for president again so that he could concentrate on achieving peace.

Johnson's withdrawal threw the Democratic Party's nomination wide open. Johnson supported his vice president, Hubert Humphrey, but McCarthy and Robert F. Kennedy were also strong contenders. When Kennedy was assassinated in June, the nation seemed out of control. And during the Democratic Convention, in Chicago, there were violent clashes between antiwar protesters and police. Humphrey was chosen, but it was not an auspicious beginning.

The Paris Peace Talks that Johnson initiated to end the Vietnam War quickly turned sour. In the end, despite Johnson's triumphant domestic accomplishments, Vietnam hung darkly over his presidency. Johnson retired to his ranch in Texas, where he wrote his memoirs. He died only four years later, on January 22, 1973.

An embattled Lyndon Johnson (right) prepares to announce to the nation that he will not seek a second term as president, on March 31, 1968. Violent opposition to the Vietnam War consumed the later years of his presidency, forcing Johnson to defend again and again a policy many Americans strongly opposed.

Johnson (below) leans on a fence at his 415-acre LBJ Ranch. Johnson's geographical identity tended to shift according to his audience. Among Southerners, he was a Southerner, but he was equally capable of claiming Texas's cattle-ranching Western heritage as his own. This "dual citizenship" was a useful political tool.

NIXON: EARLY YEARS

Born on January 9, 1913, to Frank and Hannah Nixon, Richard Milhous Nixon grew up in Yorba Linda and Whittier, California. He was a hard-working student who graduated first in his high school class of 1930. After graduating from Whittier College, Nixon went straight to law school at Duke University, graduating in 1937.

Nixon practiced law for several years, then helped start a frozen orange juice company in 1940. When that failed, he joined the Office of Price Administration, which was in charge of rationing goods during the war. Two years in this position were enough for Nixon, who disliked the inefficiency of government bureaucracy. He left to join the navy, where he served for almost four years.

Nixon resigned from the navy to run for Congress in 1946. He won by a comfortable margin, upsetting five-term incumbent Jerry Voorhis by a landslide. As a congressman, Nixon built a reputation as an aggressive anticommunist. He won national recognition as chairman of a subcommittee of the House Un-American Activities Committee (HUAC), which was investigating supposed communist spies in the government. Alger Hiss, a former State Department official, would become Richard Nixon's most famous target.

In 1950, Nixon ran for a retiring senator's seat against Helen Gahagan Douglas. By painting Mrs. Douglas, whom he dubbed "the pink lady," as a supporter of communism, Nixon won the seat.

The Nixon family (above; young Richard is far right) was not a wealthy one. Nixon's father owned a gas station and grocery store, and as a teenager, Nixon rose early each morning to buy fresh produce for the store.

Richard Nixon was born in this modest house (opposite, top) in Yorba Linda, California. He lived there until the family moved to Whittier in 1922.

Lieutenant Richard M. Nixon is seen (right, third from left) with the navy's South Pacific Combat Air Transport Command. He served with the command for slightly over a year, during 1943 and 1944. He won a citation for "meritorious and efficient performance" during this time.

THE PATH TO
THE PRESIDENCY

After little more than a year in the Senate, Nixon was chosen by President Eisenhower to be his vice-presidential running mate. Eisenhower chose Nixon, a deeply conservative Republican, to counter his own image as a moderate. But when Nixon was accused of using campaign funds improperly, Eisenhower nearly dropped him. In an attempt to persuade the nation of his innocence, Nixon gave his famous "Checkers" speech, in which he promised that he had accepted no personal gifts except for a cocker spaniel that his young daughter had named Checkers. It was enough for the nation, and for Eisenhower.

After serving as vice president for eight years, Nixon won the 1960 Republican presidential nomination. The election, in which he faced Democratic nominee John F. Kennedy, was an extremely close contest. Although Nixon began the race as an odds-on favorite, the youth and vitality of Kennedy captured the public imagination. On election day, Nixon lost by one of the narrowest margins in modern presidential history. Out of nearly 69 million votes cast, Kennedy received just 114,673 votes more than Nixon.

After his defeat in the presidential election, Nixon ran for governor of California in 1962. When he lost this race, too, he withdrew temporarily from politics to practice law in New York.

Richard Nixon weathered a remarkable number of campaigns during his political career. He ran for national office almost nonstop between 1952, when he joined Eisenhower's ticket, and 1972, when he won his second term as president. This campaign button (above) was used during his failed bid for the White House in 1960.

During the first televised presidential campaign debate (opposite, top), Vice President Nixon wore a gray suit in which he seemed to fade into the background. He also appeared unshaven, and refused to apply makeup to hide perspiration that was magnified by the television studio's bright lights. Although he looked, and performed, much better in subsequent debates, voters took greatest note of his initial appearance.

Vice President Nixon and Patricia Nixon enjoy the performance of a Ghanian dancer in March 1957 in this photograph (right). Ghana, formerly the British colony of the Gold Coast, had just become an independent country. Nixon's extensive travels as Eisenhower's vice president gave him important foreign-policy experience.

NIXON'S PRESIDENCY

In 1968, Nixon returned to politics to run for, and win, the Republican presidential nomination. As a candidate, Nixon promised to win "peace with honor" in Vietnam and to restore law and order at home. He won a narrow victory over past vice president Hubert Humphrey, the Democratic nominee, with a margin of only seventh-tenths of a percent.

In office, Nixon extended U.S. military activities into the neighboring countries of Cambodia and Laos. He also increased the aerial bombardment of North Vietnam. These policies aroused even more violent public protest. During one protest, at Ohio's Kent State University, four students were killed by National Guardsmen. Their deaths were a grim symbol of a nation tearing itself apart. But Nixon did eventually make good on his campaign promise to end the war. By August 1972, all U.S. combat troops had been withdrawn, and all U.S. involvement in Vietnam ended in January 1973.

Despite Vietnam, Nixon's most lasting achievements were in foreign policy. In February 1972, Nixon became the first U.S. president to visit China; and in June, he and Soviet leader Leonid Brezhnev signed the first SALT (Strategic Arms Limitation Talks) treaty. This treaty set limits on the nuclear buildup of each country.

Nixon swept the nation in the 1972 election, winning forty-nine states against Democratic Senator George McGovern (1922–) of South Dakota.

Although student protests like this one (right) made headlines throughout the 1960s and early 1970s, President Nixon won the 1968 election by courting the so-called "silent majority," citizens who were tired of all the protests and wanted to restore social stability.

President Nixon's visit to China (below) in February 1972 was the crowning achievement of his presidency. The United States had cut off relations with China in 1949, when communists gained control of the country. Nixon hoped to create a new international order in which several countries balanced one another, rather than allowing the world to teeter on the delicate standoff between the United States, the Soviet Union, and the People's Republic of China.

WATERGATE AND RESIGNATION

The ease of Nixon's reelection masked an ugly reality. Before the election, Nixon campaign workers had been caught breaking into the Democratic National Headquarters in the Watergate building in Washington, D.C. The object of the break-in was to uncover the Democratic presidential campaign strategy. As events unraveled, this crime led directly to the first resignation of a U.S. president.

Nixon protested his innocence of all illegal activities connected with Watergate and its coverup—activities that included illegal wiretapping, misuse of the federal government to pursue political enemies, and illegal "payoffs" to keep witnesses quiet. But when it was discovered that Nixon had taped most of his Oval Office conversations, the Supreme Court ordered the president to turn the tapes over. The tapes—one mysteriously missing eighteen minutes—greatly undermined the president's position.

Then, in August 1973, Vice President Spiro Agnew (1918–) was accused of accepting bribes both as governor of Maryland and as vice president. He resigned in disgrace and was succeeded by Gerald Ford (1913–), a congressman from Michigan.

In July 1974, the House Judiciary Committee agreed to impeach Nixon, or formally charge him with wrongdoing. Before the matter could be brought before the entire House, however, Nixon resigned, on August 9, 1974. He was the first president in history to do so.

'Simple, isn't it—Mr. President?'

On August 3, 1970, President Nixon aroused a flurry of controversy when he called serial murderer Charles Manson guilty while his case was still in trial. Although he retracted the statement almost immediately, the comment dogged him for some time. In this cartoon (above), Vice President Spiro Agnew, whose many derogatory comments about student protesters had been arousing furious commentary, instructs his boss on the delicate art of putting one's foot in one's mouth.

Nixon announced on August 8, 1974, that he would resign as president the following day. He was resigning, he said, so that America could begin a "process of healing that is so desperately needed." Standing beside Nixon (right) is his daughter, Patricia Nixon Cox, and her husband, Edward.

Although many of Nixon's associates were convicted and jailed for crimes committed during the coverup of the Watergate break-in, Nixon himself, arguably the man most responsible for the entire event, was never tried, as this poster (right) mockingly points out. He was pardoned by President Gerald Ford in September 1974 for any crimes he might have committed.

Part II

A Time of Change

The scars of the Watergate scandal ran deep in American politics. Gerald Ford's failure to win reelection can be attributed to his pardon of Richard Nixon, and likewise, Jimmy Carter's election was a rejection of traditional, Washington-trained politicians in favor of fresh faces. But Carter was unsuccessful in reshaping the office of the presidency. It was not until Ronald Reagan's election in 1980 that the office regained the power to push—and pass—significant legislation through Congress.

Ronald Reagan, the only president to serve two full terms since Dwight Eisenhower, not only restored the office of the presidency to prominence but also rebuilt a strong national identity. This happened even though Reagan, who was deeply conservative, was elected with only 51 percent of the popular vote in 1980. Many political commentators felt that Americans didn't so much agree with Reagan's beliefs as they believed in Reagan himself. This helps to explain why, after 1980, the Democrats made steady gains in Congress.

With the election of George Bush, who rode Reagan's coattails into office but lacked the same deep, personal bond with the electorate, the presidency ran head-on into a problem that Reagan's popularity had dodged. With the executive and legislative branches controlled by different parties, it was nearly impossible to achieve any sort of forward progress in domestic affairs. The federal budget deficit, gigantic when Reagan left office, spiraled to astronomical heights under the Bush administration.

Bill Clinton's election in 1992 marked a return to single party control over both Congress and the presidency.

Ronald Reagan and George Bush look poised for victory during their 1980 campaign to unseat the Democratic incumbent president, Jimmy Carter.

FORD: SUCCESSION TO THE PRESIDENCY

Leslie Lynch King, Jr., was born on July 14, 1913, to Leslie and Dorothy King in Omaha, Nebraska. His parents divorced when he was two. When his mother married Gerald Ford, Leslie Jr. was renamed Gerald Ford, Jr.

Ford grew up in the area of Grand Rapids, Michigan, attending local schools. He was a steady and hard-working boy, and graduated near the top of his high school class in 1931. Ford was a talented football player both in high school and at the University of Michigan. Although he could have pursued a professional football career, after his graduation in 1935 he coached football and boxing at Yale University. He also began attending law school there in 1938.

Ford received his law degree in 1941 and returned to Grand Rapids to practice law until the spring of 1942, when he entered the navy. He served until early 1946, mostly on a light aircraft carrier in the South Pacific, where he earned ten battle stars.

After the war, Ford returned to law practice in Grand Rapids, where he met Elizabeth Ann Bloomer Warren (1918–) in 1947. They married the following year. Soon after, Ford won the first of twelve successful campaigns for the U.S. House of Representatives.

A well-liked, moderate Republican, Ford aspired to become the Speaker of the House. In 1965 he did become minority leader, and then, in 1973, Nixon asked him to be vice president following Agnew's resignation.

Elizabeth Ann Bloomer Warren (above), known as Betty, is pictured here in about 1938. As First Lady, Betty Ford was an outspoken supporter of the Equal Rights Amendment, of the need for women on the Supreme Court, and of abortion rights. She also spoke openly about her own suffering from breast cancer, and later she talked publicly about her recovery from alcoholism and an addiction to painkillers.

Freshman congressman Gerald Ford (opposite, top) took pride in his home state of Michigan. He is seen here in the shadow of the Capitol building applying a bumper sticker that promotes Michigan apples.

On December 6, 1973, Gerald Ford was sworn in as vice president by Chief Justice Warren E. Burger (right). Nixon chose Ford in the hope that his moderate positions and strong record would make his confirmation relatively easy. Ford was the first vice president selected under the Twenty-fifth Amendment to the Constitution, which required that the president's choice to fill a vacancy be confirmed by both houses of Congress.

FORD'S PRESIDENCY

As vice president, Gerald Ford defended President Nixon's role in the Watergate scandal. Then, on August 9, 1974—only eight months after Ford became vice president—Richard Nixon became the first U.S. president ever to resign from office, and Gerald Ford became president. Ford chose Nelson Rockefeller (1908–79), the former governor of New York, as his vice president. For the first time in history, neither the vice president nor the president had been elected.

Ford took control of a country deeply shaken by the Watergate scandal. Four weeks after becoming president, in an attempt to heal the nation, Ford granted Nixon a full pardon for any crimes he might have committed. It was an extremely controversial decision. Many people felt strongly that Nixon should have stood trial, as numerous members of his staff had done. But Ford wanted the matter put to rest. He also offered clemency to draft dodgers and deserters of the Vietnam War, in another attempt to heal ugly divisions.

In addition to its political troubles, the nation Ford led was in growing economic distress. He introduced a program called Whip Inflation Now (WIN) in October 1974, but it did little to combat the growing recession.

Ford narrowly won the Republican presidential nomination in 1976. With his popularity sagging, especially because of the poor economy, he lost the general election, 48 to 50 percent, to former Georgia governor Jimmy Carter, the Democratic nominee.

Although Ford was one of the finest athletes ever to hold the presidency, he is often remembered as awkward and uncoordinated. Mrs. Ford, however, was an exceptionally graceful First Lady who had danced professionally before her marriage. In this photograph (right), the Fords are seen entering the White House Christmas dance in December, 1974.

President and Mrs. Ford campaigned down the Mississippi River on a riverboat (below) in September 1976. Ford was seriously trailing Democratic nominee Jimmy Carter as the campaign began, but he pulled almost even by election day. During a debate with Carter, Ford inaccurately stated that Poland was not under Soviet domination, a remark that hurt his campaign.

CARTER:
EARLY YEARS

James Earl Carter, Jr., was born to James and Lillian Carter on October 1, 1924, in Plains, Georgia. Jimmy excelled in school, graduating from Plains High School in 1941. His admiration for an uncle in the navy prompted him to apply to the U.S. Naval Academy, where he earned his degree in 1947. In 1948 he began training as a submarine officer, and in 1951 he became involved in nuclear-powered submarines.

When Carter's father died in 1953, Carter resigned from the navy and returned to Georgia to run the family peanut farm and warehouse. He was very successful in the peanut business, but he was also interested in local politics. In 1962 he won a seat as a Democrat in the Georgia senate, but only by proving that his opponent had committed vote fraud.

Carter's first run for governor of Georgia came in 1966, when he won third place in the Democratic primary. In 1970 he ran again, this time successfully. In his campaign, Carter portrayed himself as a conservative Democrat, but his chief legacy as governor was as a powerful advocate for civil rights.

In 1976, Carter, still an obscure, single-term governor from a relatively small state, decided to run for the presidency. His promise to restore trust between the people and the government after the Watergate scandal was appealing, and his personality and deeply rooted religious and moral convictions made fulfillment of such a promise seem possible.

A proud Ensign Carter (opposite, top) poses with his mother, Lillian, and fiancée, Rosalynn Smith, at his graduation from the U.S. Naval Academy in June 1947. Carter first attended Georgia Southwestern University and then the Georgia Institute of Technology, where he took mathematics courses needed to earn admission to the Naval Academy. Carter's class of 1943 was accelerated because of the war.

In this photograph (right), Carter holds a handful of peanuts, the product of his family's business. Although he had intended to be a career naval officer, his father's death at fifty-nine drew him back to run the peanut farm and warehouse. Carter modernized and expanded the business, eventually making himself a millionaire.

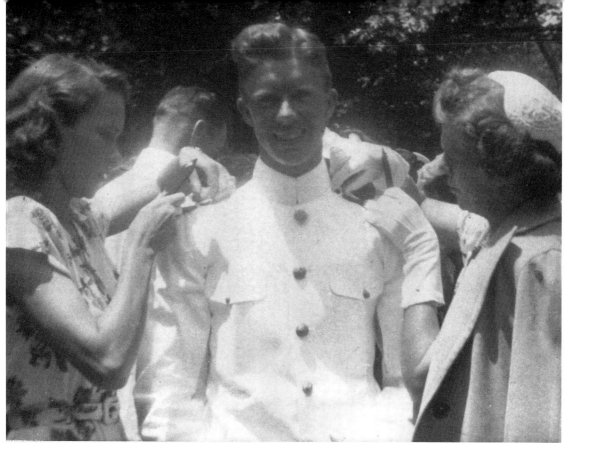

CARTER'S PRESIDENCY

Carter's easy informality, his sincerity, and his can-do grin convinced the American people that, despite his lack of experience, Carter was the best man to lead the nation in the post-Watergate era. In a close race, he won the 1976 election against incumbent president Gerald Ford.

Carter's presidential style was hands-on and personally involved. Carter's personal intervention in solving disputes between Israel and Egypt made a peace treaty between those two nations possible. Another diplomatic success was the 1977 Panama Canal Treaty, in which the United States agreed to return control of the canal to Panama in late 1999.

But the dominant domestic concern during Carter's administration was the economy. OPEC—the Oil Producing Economic Consortium of Arab nations—recognized that Western countries were almost entirely dependent on their product. With a captive market at hand, OPEC dramatically increased the price of oil: Between 1978 and 1979, the price for a single barrel of oil rose from $29 to $125—a jump of almost 500 percent. In addition to price hikes in gas and oil, the cost of other petroleum-related products—including plastics, and fabrics such as nylon and polyester—went through the roof. This drove interest rates to astonishingly high levels, past 20 percent. In the face of overwhelming international pressures, Carter was unable to stablize the economy.

In September 1978, President Carter invited Egyptian president Anwar Sadat (1918–81; left) and Israeli prime minister Menachem Begin (1914–92; right) to the presidential retreat at Camp David, Maryland (above). There, Carter personally oversaw negotiations that resulted in the first peace treaty between Israel and an Arab nation.

Some of the best-remembered moments of Carter's presidency were his attempts to make the president "one of the people." On inauguration day, he and his family walked from the Capitol building to the White House rather than ride in a limousine (right). He occasionally carried his own luggage, and once appeared in a cardigan sweater to make a national address.

CARTER'S POST-PRESIDENTIAL CAREER

Perhaps the best-remembered foreign-policy event of the Carter era was the Iranian hostage crisis. On November 4, 1979, Iranian revolutionaries captured the U.S. embassy in Teheran and took more than fifty Americans hostage.

For the next 444 days, Carter struggled to free the hostages. Virtually his entire administration was held captive by Iran. Personal qualities that had originally been advantageous—particularly his openness—now made Carter seem inadequate for the job of leading the nation in a time of trouble.

As the 1980 presidential election approached, Carter met a strong challenge by Massachusetts senator Ted Kennedy for the Democratic nomination. Although he was renominated, Carter's preoccupation with the Iranian crisis had a strong impact on his campaign. So did the terrible state of the economy. Carter lost to former California governor Ronald Reagan in a landslide—51 to 41 percent. (Most of the remaining votes went to independent candidate John Anderson.)

After leaving office, Carter returned to Georgia. He continued to be deeply concerned about human rights and was involved in international efforts to promote democracy, including the monitoring of elections in the central American country of Nicaragua. His efforts to improve his own country included work as a volunteer for Habitat for Humanity, an organization that helps to build houses for the homeless and needy.

Rosalynn Carter, posing here with her husband (above), was born in 1927 in Plains, Georgia. She and Jimmy knew each other as children and were married in 1946. As First Lady, Rosalynn was an active member of her husband's administration, sitting in on cabinet meetings and visiting other nations to promote Carter's human rights policies.

Jimmy Carter aged visibly during his four years in office (opposite, top). Though his trademark grin never left him, this serious, worried look became especially familiar to Americans during the Iranian hostage crisis.

Although Carter left office as one of the most unpopular presidents in history (during the second oil crisis, his popularity rating dropped below Richard Nixon's), he became one of the nation's most successful and active ex-presidents. In this photograph (right), Carter is seen helping in a neighborhood effort in Atlanta to build housing for the homeless.

REAGAN: EARLY YEARS

Ronald Wilson Reagan was born on February 6, 1911, to John and Nelle Reagan in Tampico, Illinois. Reagan's father, an alcoholic, was never a successful businessman, and the family moved several times with each new job. The Reagans eventually settled in Dixon, Illinois, where Reagan graduated from high school in 1928. More interested in sports and drama than in academics, Reagan graduated from Eureka College in 1932. After college, he began his career as a radio sports broadcaster in Des Moines, Iowa.

In 1937, Reagan had a successful screen test with Warner Brothers and signed a seven-year contract with the company. The studio liked his cheerful good humor and his all-American looks. In 1940, Reagan married actress Jane Wyman, but the couple divorced in 1948.

World War II interrupted Reagan's blossoming career. He served in the army from 1942 to 1945, although poor vision kept him out of combat. When he returned from the war, his film career had lost its momentum. Nonetheless, Reagan served as president of the Screen Actors Guild from 1947 to 1952 and again from 1959 to 1960. (The Screen Actors Guild was a union that lobbied for better contracts and improved working conditions for movie actors.) In 1952, he remarried, this time to actress Nancy Davis (1923–). In 1954, Reagan moved to television as host of "General Electric Theatre," where he remained until 1962.

Ronald Reagan (second row, first on left), and the rest of the third-grade class of Tampico, Illinois, pose for the camera in this group portrait (right). From the time Reagan was born until he was nine, his family moved five times, eventually settling in Dixon, Illinois.

Reagan began his career in broadcasting as a sports announcer for a Davenport, Iowa, radio station. His rise to fame began, however, after he moved to radio WHO, in Des Moines, where he became a local celebrity as the major league baseball and college football announcer. Here (opposite, bottom) Reagan is shown during a broadcast.

Nancy Reagan (below) presents her husband with a "proud Papa" award on the birth of their first child, Patricia (Patti), in 1952. Reagan had four children: Maureen, by his first wife, Jane Wyman; Michael, adopted with Wyman; and Patti and Ron Jr., with Nancy. Although as president Reagan was a vigorous advocate for traditional family values, his own family was not a particularly close or traditional one.

GOVERNOR AND CANDIDATE

During the 1950s, Reagan underwent a political transformation from a liberal Democrat to a conservative Republican. He began his political career in 1964 by working for Barry Goldwater's presidential campaign. Two years later, he ran for governor of California, an office he won with 58 percent of the vote. He ran again in 1970, winning with 53 percent this time.

Reagan's most notable actions as governor were to cut the size of the state government, eliminate the budget deficit, and reform the welfare system. He was a candidate for the 1968 Republican presidential nomination, but lost to Richard Nixon.

In 1975, having served two terms as governor, Reagan again sought the Republican presidential nomination. He nearly won, a remarkable feat since he had challenged an incumbent president, Gerald Ford. He spent the late 1970s building support for his conservative platform, and in 1980 he finally won his party's nomination.

In his campaign against incumbent president Jimmy Carter, Reagan asked the famous question, "Are you better off than you were four years ago?" Voters answered by granting Reagan a landslide victory over Carter.

Ronald Reagan proudly cast his first vote for president for Franklin D. Roosevelt in 1932, and remained a loyal Democrat until 1960. By 1964, however, he had become convinced that a large central government sapped the national spirit. In this 1966 photo (right), Reagan speaks to the National Press Club during his successful campaign for governor of California, the office in which he first implemented his "less-is-more" platform of government.

Ronald and Nancy Reagan are the stars during this festive campaign stop during his successful 1980 bid for the presidency (below). Both as a candidate and as president, Reagan's talent for public speaking—honed as a radio broadcaster and actor—was a great advantage, earning him the nickname "the Great Communicator."

REAGAN'S FIRST TERM

Only hours after Ronald Reagan took office on January 20, 1981, the Iranian hostages were released, under terms fiercely negotiated by outgoing president Jimmy Carter. Then, on March 30, 1981, Reagan was shot and seriously wounded by John Hinckley, Jr. His quick recovery, however, averted any crisis in the presidency.

Reagan believed that cutting taxes on industry and on the wealthier portion of Americans would stimulate a demand for products and lead to a stronger economy. In August 1981, Reagan signed the largest tax cut in history. He also wanted to lower inflation, which was at 13 percent when he took office. This he did, but with painful results. Unemployment rose to almost 11 percent before the economy began to recover in late 1982.

Reagan's approach to foreign affairs was equally revolutionary. With a motto of "peace through strength," Reagan initiated a dramatic increase in defense spending. Reagan's strategy was to try to bankrupt the Soviet Union by forcing it to keep up with U.S. defense developments.

Reagan's other great foreign-affairs interest was Nicaragua, whose Sandinista government he considered to be one step away from communism. One of his first acts as president was to cut off aid to Nicaragua. Under Reagan, the United States gave aid to the contras, or rebels, who were trying to overthrow the Sandinistas.

David Stockman (above) was Reagan's first director of the Office of Management and Budget, a position in which Stockman oversaw the implementation of Reagan's tax cuts. In a controversial 1981 interview with The Atlantic Monthly *magazine, however, Stockman expressed concerns about Reagan's economic program and even about his own calculations. His concerns, particularly about the federal deficit, were ignored, and he resigned in 1985.*

Preventing communism from spreading to Central America was one of Reagan's consuming passions as president. But after CIA activity against the Nicaraguan Sandinistas was discovered—including the mining of Nicaragua's harbors—Congress banned Reagan from aiding their opponents, the contras. His administration's efforts to overcome this ban resulted in the Iran-contra scandal of 1985. Reagan is shown here meeting with contra leaders in the cabinet room of the White House (right).

President and Mrs. Reagan (right) were a close couple, both publicly and privately. As First Lady, Nancy Reagan was criticized for exercising too much influence over her husband's decisions. Revelations that she had altered the president's schedule after consultation with an astrologer did little to reassure the public.

REAGAN: SECOND TERM

Reagan won the 1984 Republican presidential nomination with little difficulty, trouncing Democratic candidate Walter Mondale (1928–), who openly admitted that he would raise taxes. The economy played a big part in Reagan's victory. It had fully recovered by 1984 and continued to boom throughout his second term.

In 1985, Mikhail Gorbachev (1931–) took power in the Soviet Union. Gorbachev, the youngest and most flexible Soviet leader in decades, made a new relationship with the Soviet Union possible. In 1987, he and Reagan signed the Intermediate-Range Nuclear Forces treaty, the first treaty ever to agree to destroy nuclear weapons.

Reagan vowed repeatedly that he would never make deals with international terrorists. In 1985, however, his administration secretly agreed to sell weapons to Iran in return for help freeing the hostages. Some of the money from Iran was then channeled to the Nicaraguan contras, whom Congress had forbidden the president to aid.

When these actions were made public, "Iran-contra" became the worst scandal since Watergate. While Reagan was never directly linked to any illegal acts, his loose control of his staff lost him considerable respect.

Despite this cloud, Reagan retired to California as a tremendously popular president. But the Reagan Revolution also left lingering problems. "Reaganomics" had created an enormous budget deficit, a problem that would plague Reagan's vice president and successor, George Bush.

Reagan first met Soviet leader Mikhail Gorbachev (right) in Geneva in November 1985. It had been six years since the last U.S.-Soviet summit, but these two leaders met again in Reykjavik, Iceland, less than a year later. On December 8, 1987, they met a final time in Washington, D.C., to sign a historic arms-control treaty. The open and friendly relationship between these two superpower leaders did much to ease East-West tensions.

The Reagans officially retired to Bel Air, California, but they spent much time at Rancho de Cielo, the 688-acre ranch outside Santa Barbara, California (below), which Reagan bought in 1974. Despite his age (seventy-eight upon leaving office), Reagan enjoyed the hard physical labor of ranch work throughout his presidency.

BUSH:
EARLY YEARS

George Herbert Walker Bush was born on June 12, 1924, in Milton, Massachusetts, to Prescott and Dorothy Bush. The Bushes moved soon after George's birth to Greenwich, Connecticut, where George grew up, the second of five children. Bush's father was a successful investment banker and later a respected senator from Connecticut. Though the family enjoyed every material advantage, the Bush children were taught that their privileges carried the obligation to help others.

Bush attended private schools, graduating from Phillips Andover Academy in 1942. He put off college to enroll in the navy on his eighteenth birthday. Bush earned his pilot's wings a year later, becoming the youngest pilot in the navy, and flew fifty-eight combat missions during World War II. In January 1945, Bush married Barbara Pierce (1925–), whom he had met at a dance in 1942. The couple claimed to have fallen instantly in love, and were secretly engaged in 1943.

After the war, Bush attended Yale, where he captained the baseball team and graduated with honors in 1948. After college, he left the East Coast for Texas, where he entered the oil business. In 1966 Bush sold his oil interests for $1 million and devoted himself to politics.

George Bush was born in this gracious Victorian house (right) in Milton, Massachusetts. Although as a national politician Bush proclaimed himself a Texan, he was a New Englander by upbringing. Born in Massachusetts, he grew up in Greenwich, Connecticut, and spent his summers at a family house in Kennebunkport, Maine.

Lieutenant George Bush in 1944 is seen here aboard his single-engined VT-51 Avenger (opposite, bottom), named Barbara, for his future wife. Bush—one of only four of his original squadron of fourteen to survive the war—won a Distinguished Flying Cross for a September 1944 mission in which he was hit by enemy fire but managed to complete his mission before bailing out of his wrecked aircraft. He was rescued at sea by a submarine.

George Bush poses for the Yale yearbook (below). Although he dons a baseball uniform, he is listed as "Captain" Bush, a reference to his military service in Wold War II.

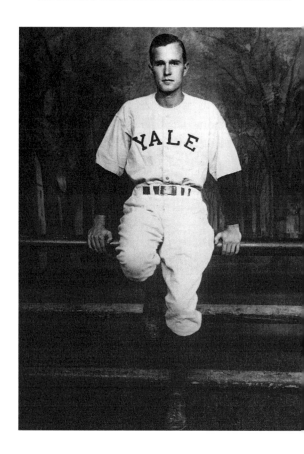

BUSH:
A VARIED CAREER

Bush's political career began in 1952, when he campaigned in Houston for Dwight Eisenhower. In 1964, he won the Republican nomination to challenge a strong incumbent Democratic senator, Ralph W. Yarborough. To no one's surprise, he lost.

Two years later, however, Bush won a seat in the U.S. House of Representatives as a moderate Republican, and he was easily reelected two years later. In 1970, Bush made a second run for the Senate, sacrificing his safe seat in the House in an effort to win the Senate seat for the Republicans. When he lost, President Nixon appointed him to the United Nations, where he spent nearly two years. Nixon next named Bush head of the Republican Party, giving him, as it happened, the problem of leading the party through the Watergate scandal.

President Ford appointed Bush representative to China. A year later, Ford asked him to head the Central Intelligence Agency. Despite his short term—not quite a year—Bush is remembered as one of the agency's best directors.

Bush lost the 1980 Republican nomination to Ronald Reagan, despite a strong early showing. Although Bush had attacked Reagan's economic program as "voodoo economics," Reagan chose him as his running mate. Together they swept the nation in both 1980 and 1984. Bush was a loyal vice president who traveled widely and supported Reagan's position without fail.

His experience in China as chief of the U.S. Liaison Office left a deep mark on George Bush. While president, he consistently supported China's leaders even after they massacred pro-democracy protesters in Tiananmen Square in June 1989. Bush is shown in this photograph (right) bicycling with his wife, Barbara, in the Chinese capital of Beijing.

The two vice-presidential candidates—Vice President Bush and New York representative Geraldine Ferraro—debate during the 1984 campaign (opposite, bottom).

Bush (below) served four years as the U.S. representative for the seventh district of Texas. His most remarkable action as a congressman was to vote in favor of the 1968 Civil Rights Act, even though his district strongly opposed it.

BUSH'S PRESIDENCY

Despite his extremely strong credentials, Vice President Bush faced a tough fight from Senator Robert Dole of Kansas for the 1988 Republican presidential nomination. He won the slot, and continued to a landslide victory against Massachusetts governor Michael Dukakis (1933–), the Democratic nominee.

At heart, Bush was a moderate Republican who, like Eisenhower, was not interested in any bold domestic reforms. Instead, he concentrated on foreign policy, especially on the formation of a "new world order" following the fall of communism in the Soviet Union and Eastern Europe.

Bush did not hesitate to use military power to achieve his objectives. His defining act as president was to organize and lead a multinational coalition to oppose Iraq's invasion of Kuwait in August 1990. Bush was famous for his personal diplomacy, and this skill was key in winning the participation of several Arab nations—most notably Saudi Arabia and Syria—making massive military intervention in the region more acceptable to the Arab world.

By the end of the Persian Gulf War—named "Operation Desert Storm" by military officials—President Bush enjoyed unprecedented popularity. But his popularity, as for most presidents, was closely tied to the economy. A recession that had begun in 1990 dragged on into 1992, giving his opponents one of many powerful campaign weapons. After his loss to Arkansas governor Bill Clinton (1946–), Bush retired to Texas.

President and Mrs. Bush greet the crowds at his inaugural parade (right), on January 20, 1989. Some felt that Barbara Bush's grandmotherly image was a great asset to her husband during his presidency. Her efforts as First Lady, including a campaign to stamp out adult illiteracy, seemed directed at fulfilling Bush's promise to create a "kinder, gentler nation."

President Bush was in his element as commander in chief during the Persian Gulf War. He shares a meal with troops (below) during a Thanksgiving visit to Saudi Arabia.

CLINTON: EARLY YEARS

Bill Clinton was born William Jefferson Blythe IV in Hope, Arkansas, on August 19, 1946. His father, William, died in a car crash before Bill was born. Clinton's mother, Virginia Cassidy Blythe, married Roger Clinton in 1950 and the family moved to Hot Springs in 1952.

Clinton was ambitious from the start. An exceptional student, he graduated from Georgetown University in 1968. He then attended England's Oxford University on a prestigious Rhodes scholarship before entering Yale Law School. Clinton earned his law degree in 1973 and returned to Arkansas, where in 1974 he made his first bid for political office—an unsuccessful campaign for the House of Representatives. In 1975, Clinton married Hillary Rodham (1948–), a Yale classmate.

Clinton's political career began in earnest with his election as Arkansas attorney general in 1976. After only one two-year term, he was elected governor at the remarkable age of thirty-two. Politically inexperienced, the young governor lost his first bid for reelection, in 1980, but was elected again in 1982 to the second of his five terms as governor.

By 1992, Democrats were hungry for the White House, having been shut out of the executive branch for twelve years. Of the six Democrats who declared their candidacy for president, Governor Bill Clinton of Arkansas quickly emerged as the front-runner.

A beaming Bill Clinton (above) celebrates his graduation from Hot Springs High School in 1964.

This photograph (opposite, top) shows Bill Clinton campaigning for governor of his home state. He won by emphasizing education, welfare reform, and business development. Clinton earned a national reputation by chairing the National Governors Association and by working hard for several federal reforms, including President Bush's National Education Goals.

Bill Clinton (right) first achieved national prominence as a founding member of the Democratic Leadership Council. Clinton argued that the Democrats would never regain the White House unless they could win back the confidence of the "Reagan Democrats," middle class Americans who believed the Democratic leadership catered to liberal "special interest groups"—including minorities and homosexuals—at the expense of "ordinary" Americans.

CLINTON'S CAMPAIGN AND FIRST 100 DAYS

Bill Clinton's central campaign theme was change: He promised change from twelve years of "trickle-down" economics, the program started by Reagan that Democrats credited with ruining the economy. He also pledged change in, among other things, the nation's health care system. Clinton achieved an electoral landslide victory over Bush. A third candidate, Texas billionaire Ross Perot, captured 19 percent of the popular vote but failed to win a single state in the electoral college.

Once in office, Clinton proposed lifting a ban preventing admitted homosexuals from serving in the military. The proposal stirred controversy in the armed forces and the public. Clinton also introduced his plan to aid the country's economy, sparking more debate. Some Republicans charged that Clinton was offering what, as they saw it, Democrats had always offered: large, expensive government programs funded by tax increases, but many Democrats defended the plan as a bold approach towards future prosperity.

To carry out the task of health care reform, Clinton appointed First Lady Hillary Rodham Clinton as head of a special committee. It was a move unprecedented in the history of the presidency. Like the economic program and the attempt to lift the ban on homosexuals, it prompted many to debate whether or not, as the country moved toward the twenty-first century, the American presidency had truly entered a time of change.

Bill Clinton and his running mate, Senator Albert Gore of Tennessee (1948–), brought a new generation into the White House. The ticket's youth and vigor captured the public imagination at a time when the country was looking for a change from "business-as-usual" in Washington. The team toured the nation by bus (right) to show that they, in contrast to President Bush, were in touch with ordinary Americans.

In what will become a trademark of his presidential style, Bill Clinton warmly embraces the African-American poet Maya Angelou at his inauguration on January 21, 1993. Clinton had commissioned Angelou to write a poem for his inauguration that would speak to all Americans. Angelou was the first woman—and African American—to receive such an honor.

Hillary Rodham Clinton and first daughter Chelsea (below) share a proud moment at the Clinton inaugural. During the campaign, Mrs. Clinton, a prominent lawyer and political activist, had come under fire when she remarked that some of the public would ". . . rather I'd stayed home and baked cookies and had teas instead of a career." The Republican Party leapt on this remark as an insult to traditional values, but it failed to change the course of the campaign, or of Mrs. Clinton's independent views.

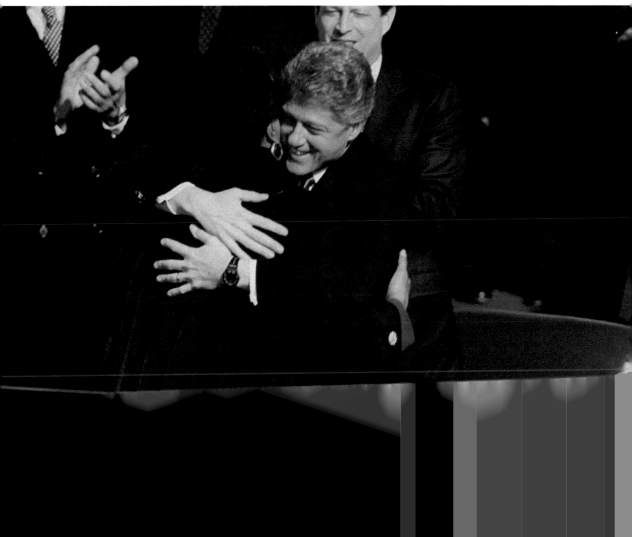

Resource Guide

Key to picture locations within the Library of Congress collections (and where available, photo negative numbers): P - Prints and Photographs Division; R - Rare Book Division; G - General Collections; MSS - Manuscript Division; G&M - Geography Division
Other sources: AC - Architect of the Capitol; CC - Clinton Campaign; DEL - Dwight Eisenhower Library; GFL - Gerald Ford Library; HTL - Harry Truman Library; JCL - Jimmy Carter Library; JFKL - John F. Kennedy Library; LBJL - Lyndon B. Johnson Library; NA - National Archives; RNL - Richard Nixon Library; RRL - Ronald Reagan Library; USGS - U.S. Geological Survey; WH - White House Photo Dept.

PICTURES IN THIS VOLUME

2–3 Capitol, AC 4–5 Carter button, JCL 6–7 Truman, P 8–9 Map, USGS

Timeline: 10–11 Truman, P, USZ62-70080; airlift, NA 12–13 Kennedy, JFKL; Martin Luther King, Jr., P 14–15 Impeach Nixon, NA; hostages, NA 16–17 Sandra Day O'Connor, P; marines, NA

Part I: 18–19 Nixon, WH 20–21 Truman as boy, P, USZ62-86675; soldier, P, USZ62-58106; family farm, HTL 22–23 Bess Truman, P, USZ62-25813; Truman w/FDR, HTL; Truman, HTL 24–25 cartoon, P, USZ62-16778; Potsdam, P 26–27 MacArthur, P; cartoon, P, USZ62-86585 28–29 McCarthy, P, USZ62-101382; House committee, P; family, HTL; Truman & Jack Benny, HTL 30–31 license, DEL; camping, DEL; graduate, DEL 32–33 cartoon, P, USZ62-13640; soldiers, P, USZ62-25600 34–35 Mamie Eisenhower, P, USZ62-51913; airport, DEL; button, DEL 36–37 Ike greeting JFK, DEL; family, DEL 38–39 young Kennedy, JFKL; family, JFKL; gunboat, JFKL 40–41 inaugural, P; convention, P, LC U9-4667-HH; wedding, P, LC F-02-S309-36-12 42–43 Jackie Kennedy, P, USZ62-23271; Khrushchev, P; sign, P, USZ62-92297 44–45 brothers, JFKL; Teamster hearing, FJKL 46–47 funeral, JFKL; Oswald, P, LC-U9-18184-35; Jackie & Bobby Kennedy, JFKL 48–49 young LBJ, LBJL; school portrait, LBJL; teachers certificate, LBJL 50–51 Lady Bird Johnson, P; swearing-in ceremony, P;

M. L. King, Jr., P 52–53 Vietnam, P, LC U9-13957-4; protest, P, LC U9-11386-11 54–55 TV announcement, LBJL; ranch, LBJL 56–57 Nixon family, RNL; birthplace, P, USZ62-42298; Nixon in Pacific, P 58–59 debate, P, U9-5082-4; African trip, P, USZ62-852210; button, RNL 60–61 student protests, P, LC U9-22657-5; Nixon in China, P 62–63 cartoon, P, USZ62-95511; poster, P; resignation speech, P

Part II: 64–65 Reagan & Bush, RRL 66–67 young Betty Ford, GFL; congressman, GFL; swearing in, P 68–69 campaign, GFL; Christmas dance, P, LC-U9-30581-14 70–71 graduation, JCL; Carter, JCL; 72–73 Camp David, JCL; inaugural parade, JCL 74–75 Jimmy & Rosalynn, WH; Carter, WH; Habitat for Humanity, JCL 76–77 Ron & Nancy, P, USZ62-7980-5; 3rd grade class, RRL; radio announcer, RRL 78–79 Reagan speech, P, LC U9-16048-12; campaign, RRL 80–81 Stockman, WH; Ron & Nancy, WH; contras, RRL 82–83 Gorbechev, WH; Reagan on ranch, RRL 84–85 Bush at Yale, WH; pilot, WH; childhood home, WH 86–87 congressman, P, LC U9-22655-36; Bush in China, WH; debate, P 88–89 inaugural parade, WH; Gulf War, WH 90–91 graduate, CC; campaign, CC; Clinton, CC 92–93 Hillary & Chelsea, AC; Clinton & Al Gore, CC; Clinton hug, AC

SUGGESTED READING

BLASSINGAME, WYATT. *The Look-It-Up Book of Presidents.* New York: Random House, 1984
DEGREGORIO, W. A. *The Complete Book of U.S. Presidents.* New York: Dembner Books, 1991.
MILKIS, Sidney M., Nelson, Michael. *The American Presidency: Origins and Developments.*

Washington, DC: Congressional Quarterly Press, 1990
WESTERFELD, Scott. *Watergate.* Englewood Cliffs, NJ: Silver Burdett Press, Inc., 1991
WHITNEY, D. C. *The American Presidents,* 6th ed. New York: Doubleday, 1986.

Index

Page numbers in *italics* indicate illustrations